"My Unspoken Truth"

By:

Vernisa Smith

Table of Content

Chapter 1

THE ROMANCE

One warm, sunny evening my friends called and wanted to go out. I did not want to go, but consented due to their persistence. We went out to happy hour and after arriving there, I was so glad I went. I really needed the night out and I had no idea what was waiting there for me. The music sounded great and was energizing, the food was delicious and the ambiance was very soothing. As people were dancing and having drinks a gentleman approached our table and asked me if I would like to dance. Looking at his tall, dark and handsome stature I answered "why yes".

After the dance, he escorted me back to my table and we introduced ourselves to each other.

His name was Hamilton and I told him my name was Simone. Hamilton joined us at the table and I introduced him to my friends, Brenda and Mildred. Hamilton went on to explain that he and his friends were there for a two-day conference and he was happy they had decided to stay for happy hour. Hamilton said he and his friends saw us when we walked in and admitted that to his friends he had said "The young lady with the gray on has class." He was referring to me. One of his friends had commented that my girlfriend had big boobs.

That comment he could have kept between him and his friend. While engaging in a great conversation, Hamilton and I sought to learn more about each other. As we talked, I discovered that he had two girls and I shared with him that I had a son.

Before leaving that evening, we exchanged phone numbers and began talking over the phone for hours at a time, like teenagers. We talked about everything from food to sports.

After about two weeks of enjoying communicating over the phone, we made plans to go out on a date. We went out to eat dinner and then ended the evening by going to see a movie. Hamilton and I found that we had so much in common. He loved sports and so did I. He couldn't believe I loved and knew so much about sports. A wonderful cook, he would often cook and invite me over for dinner to share his expertise on the grill. People always say that the way to a man's heart is through his stomach, but I think he tried to get to my heart through my stomach. His food was so good to me. The more we got to know each other, the more relaxed we became around each other.

Hamilton and I both liked to travel and before long, we started going out of town a lot, meeting his friends and going to parties. He seemed to be a very nice man and we were having a wonderful time together. Hamilton put forth the effort to get to know my son as well and Andre was always included in our activities.

A single woman with kids always wants to know that the man she is dating accepts her kids and will be good to them. Hamilton was so kind and gentle and seemed so loving. He appeared to be a good man and made me feel special.

Both Hamilton and I were divorced and it had been just my son and me for a long time. We lived in an apartment and Andre was pretty much confined to being inside and had gotten content with not playing outside.

As a result, whenever Andre and I went over to Hamilton's house to visit, he never liked to go outside. When Hamilton initially took Andre outside, he cried emphatically, "I don't want to go outside; those flies might try to bite me." Hamilton and I laughed. I had sheltered my poor baby to the point where he thought flies would bite.

The more we visited, the more comfortable Andre became with going outside. He met a friend in the neighborhood named Cortez and they started playing football and having fun in the yard together. Andre quickly forgot about the flies. I eventually introduced Hamilton to my mother, who lived in the same apartment community in which I lived. She seemed to think he was a nice man. As we grew closer, Hamilton and I began to travel a lot with his job.

He was working and he brought me along; we had the evenings when he was not in meetings and seminars to sightsee. We attended many conferences and traveled many other places. I enjoyed spending time with him and became more and more fond of him.

Chapter 2

THE UNEXPECTED

One morning, while at work, I bent down to pick up some boxes and I got light headed. I went to the lab and had a urinalysis run and found out that I was pregnant. Hamilton and I had been dating for a year. Right away, I called my Ob/Gyn and made an appointment. After telling Hamilton, he expressed a desire to go to the appointment with me; we found out it was true and we were going to have a baby. After leaving the doctor's office, we were driving along in the car and a song came on the radio.

"Somebody Loves You Baby," He sang along and told me, "somebody loves you baby."

I was expecting with child. Hamilton seemed very happy about the idea of the two of us having a baby together. He told me he wanted me to eat lots of fish so his child will be smart. It has always been said that eating fish while pregnant makes the child smart, but who really knows if that actually works?

Hamilton introduced me to his two daughters, Shay and Felicia. They were both beautiful and very sweet girls. I felt that they were genuine and we got along very well. I also had the pleasure of meeting his sister, Dorothy; His two brothers, Roosevelt who lived out of town and Jerome, whom was local. Hamilton lost his parents at a young age, so he had a close relationship with his siblings. Hamilton went to all of my Dr. visits with me. I noticed just a small change in Hamilton when I was about four months pregnant. At this particular visit the Dr. gave me a prescription to have filled.

On the way to the pharmacy, Hamilton and I were arguing and he called me a witch. I was stunned that he would even have the audacity to call me out of my name. I shook it off and pulled myself together and I went inside to the pharmacy. To my surprise, when I came out, he was gone. He had left me there without a ride. I called him to ask where he was and he told me to catch a bus or call a cab. He said that he didn't have time for this crap. I wanted to cry, I was so embarrassed. Here I was, four months pregnant with his child and he leaves me stranded at the pharmacy. He seemed to have no remorse about leaving me there. I didn't even think the argument was that serious. I called his sister, Dorothy, to pick me up. She came and said nothing about having to pick me up. I didn't let my mother know what he had done, I was too embarrassed and I did not want to create any issues.

Later that night, there was a knock at the door and it was Hamilton. He had come by to say he was sorry and he didn't want me to be upset. He wanted me to be happy throughout my pregnancy. He apologized and I accepted. I told him that his actions and harsh words had taken me by surprise, not to mention that he had hurt my feelings. Something I was not expecting, especially from him. Some would say, this was a huge red flag and I should have seen it. I was hurt, but I let this incident go because we were arguing and it just got out of hand. After all, he did apologize. Maybe he was just a little stressed about the new baby coming, right?

Eventually Hamilton said that he wanted Andre and me to move in with him. I told him I wanted to wait until the baby was born so I suggested that, in the meantime, we make some upgrades to his house.

I told him that once we finish the house and the baby is born, we will move in. As part of the plan, we began buying what was needed in order to get started working on the house. We purchased new carpet, new kitchen cabinets and began remodeling the bathrooms and painting all the rooms in the house. It took about four months to complete the process of upgrading the house. During this time, his sister Dorothy was preparing for her wedding coming up in the same year in which our baby was due.

By June, I was five months pregnant and Hamilton and I started having arguments regularly. He was not coming by as often and when he did come around, he treated me as if he resented the fact that I was pregnant with his child. He would get angry and not call for several days and as a result, I began to feel neglected.

I couldn't understand what was wrong, what I had done to make him act this way towards me. I took a lot of verbal abuse from him during this time as well. He had begun to show me some inconsistencies in his behavior the kind of things I didn't want to see in a man with whom I was in relationship. I just thought he was stressed and so was I and things will settle down once the baby is born. Yet, another red flag that I chose to make excuses for and overlook.

Finally, October rolled around and Dorothy was making the final preparations for her wedding. Everyone was excited and was working diligently to make sure that everything was ready. Hamilton, along with his two daughters, Shay and Felicia and his brother, Roosevelt, were all a part of the wedding party. The day before the wedding, Hamilton took me shopping to finish getting my lingerie.

We argued the entire time we were shopping. I had no idea why the arguing even started. It had to be something petty. It seemed as though all we did together, while I was pregnant, was argued; we argued about this, that and everything else. Later on that evening, we went over to Dorothy's house. The entire family was there to celebrate with her and share the last night with her as a single woman, as the wedding was the next day.

Hamilton suggested that he, his brothers and his cousins go out to a club and he asked his brother, Jerome, to take me home. I told him that I wanted him to take me home, instead of his brother taking me. Hamilton was not happy about my request and he   let everyone know it with his actions. He grudgingly drove me home and did not help me out of the car nor help me to the door. He drove off as soon as I exited the car. Yet another raised eye brow.

Is this the type of man he really is? Stress should not make you act out of character this often.

On the day of the wedding, he picked me up to get dressed for the wedding at his house. Two of his cousins had spent the night at his house and were getting dressed there as well. Hamilton seemed to be calm and was in a much better mood than he had been recently. He had given me his car to use. This ensured that I would have transportation to get back and forth to work and take my son, Andre to school. After the wedding ceremony, I waited around while the wedding party took pictures and later we headed to the reception. The day had been going well and the reception was going along just fine until later, when everyone began to dance. Instead of Hamilton dancing with me, he acted as if I was not there and asked another woman to dance. He ignored me all night and treated me as if we were not together.

None of this was good for me because I already felt fat and pregnant and he was treating me as if he was ashamed to be with me. Finally, when the time came for the bride and groom to depart, Hamilton was preparing to take them to their Hotel. He never asked me to come and had made no arrangements for me to get home. Everyone had begun to leave and if I had not gotten up and gone outside, I would probably have been left there alone. I asked Hamilton if he was going to leave me and he said that he was going to come back for me. I asked him why I could not just ride with him to drop them off as well. He looked at me strangely and it was clear that he did not want me to come, but he allowed me to get in the van. He was angry and we argued all the way to the hotel. He never minded arguing in front of his family. I'm sure they did not want to hear us arguing on their wedding night.

They had just said "I Do" and were happy and there we were spoiling the mood. I told him how low down he was for treating me so badly at the reception and for trying to leave me there without saying a word. He started cursing me out in front of his sister and brother-in-law. We dropped them off and then he dropped me off at home. I did not hear from him until the following night. I asked Hamilton why he didn't call me and he said that he wanted some time to himself and had gone out with his cousins, who were still in town. He had taken his car, so I was stuck at my apartment with no transportation. I was fortunate that my son was away at his father's house for the weekend.

A few days later, Hamilton came over and I told him that I was getting very tired of him neglecting me. In order to pacify me he gave me his car back so I would have transportation and he drove his truck.

One evening, I had gone to my mother's house to visit her. I was just sitting and talking with her; it was the middle of August and I was seven months pregnant. After some time, I told her I was going to head home and as I was driving out of her subdivision, I saw some kids from afar playing. They were running back and forth in the street. I questioned why they were playing in the middle of the street and I noticed a bus coming in the other direction. The three of them were running back and forth across the street, as if they were trying to beat the bus. As I was approaching them, I was wondering what they were doing. All of a sudden, out of nowhere one of the three young guys ran into the car. His body hit the windshield so hard that it shattered and he literally almost hit me in my face. Instead he bounced off the windshield and hit the right side of the car, before smashing to the ground. I was screaming hysterically!

All I could say was "Lord help me! Lord help me!"

I was panicked and completely out of control and could not move. There was a woman sitting on her porch and she ran over and began to pray with me. Next, a gentleman ran over to the car. He asked if I was ok and proceeded to try to get me to calm down. When the police and the ambulance arrived, I was still unable to get out of the car. Eventually, the gentleman moved back from the car and the police asked me to put the car in park. Finally, they got me out of the car. I gave him the phone number and asked the gentleman if he would please call my mother. My mother was not far and it did not take her long to arrive at the scene.

She ran over to me and with a look of concern she said "Simone, what happened?"

I wept and said "I was driving and this young guy ran into the car. I never saw him coming; His body just ran into my windshield and hit the right side of the car before bouncing off and hitting the ground. I explained that it all happened so fast and it was an accident. I don't know how he looked because I was never able to see his face."

My mother repeatedly told me to calm down, she said I was making myself more upset and it was not good for the baby. I was so afraid and concerned for him. Until this day, I have never seen him. They took the young guy to the hospital in an ambulance. The gentleman that stayed with me took me to the ER at Brookwood Hospital. I was seven months pregnant and no one wanted me to take any chances with the baby or me. My girlfriend came and took Hamilton's car to my grandmother's house and parked it in her back yard.

My nerves were shot and I could not stop shaking. I am not sure that I knew the magnitude of the impact at that time. The car was damaged and clearly showed that I had been hit by something. I asked the gentleman how the young guy looked that hit me and he wouldn't tell me. He just kept avoiding my questions about the young man. He was so kind and patient with my mother and me and stayed with us after taking us to the ER. After I was examined by the Dr., they assured me that the baby was fine and was still in good health. Although the baby was fine, I was still very upset and it was clear to the doctor that I would need something to help me relax. Before releasing me, the doctor gave me a sedative and sent me home with a prescription for pills to help me sleep. The gentleman remained by my side and assisted my mother and me to her house and helped us inside.

He stayed and talked to my mother for a while. He was a very kind gentleman and I certainly appreciated him being there. He had witnessed the accident and was the first person to come to my aid at the scene. I don't know what I would have done had he not been there at my side, through the whole ordeal.

My mother was finally able to reach Hamilton by phone and she told him that I had been in a car accident. He and his sister came over immediately. He expressed that he had no idea that I had been in an accident but had been wondering where I was because I had not yet arrived home.

He had been looking for me and said to his sister, "Simone should have been here by now." He proceeded to ask what happened and where his car was.

I was heavily sedated, so my mother told him about the accident. She explained what happened and told him that his car was parked at my grandmother's house. After some time, Hamilton and his sister left. He returned the next day and apologized to me expressing that he did not know the accident had been that serious, until he saw how bad his car looked. My mother stayed with me and took care of me and my affairs. She called my supervisor at work and explained that I had been in an accident and that I was told by my doctor that I would not be able to return to work until the following Monday. A week passed and I was adamant about going to see the young man that hit me.

He was still in the hospital due to trauma to the head. Hamilton and I went to the hospital. I thought I was emotionally ready and would be able to go in.

Unfortunately, I made it as far as the double doors just outside of his hallway and was unable to go in. As a result of my not going in, I was never able to actually see him. Hamilton proceeded to go in without me and would give me an account of his health. Hamilton was back there for what seemed to be an eternity and as I waited, I tried to relax.

When Hamilton finally reappeared, his eyes were filled with tears. I asked "How is he doing?" Hamilton never uttered a word, but only shook his head and bowed it sadly. This was not the report I was looking for and I was saddened. I asked Hamilton to take me to visit the young man's parents and he consented.

I felt that I needed to do something to let them know that I cared. After finding out where they lived, He asked me if I was sure that this was what I wanted to do.

He seemed skeptical, but I assured him that I was sure and he drove me to their home.

We arrived at their home and after visiting and talking with them for a short while, we got up to leave. I gave them my phone number and told them that they were welcome to call me at any time. I made myself available to them and this proved to be a big mistake. The young man's father asked me if we could give them money to go to the hospital to see their son. They began to call me on my job everyday asking me for money that I did not have. I took this on as my issue and made it my duty to call the hospital each day and night. I wanted to keep up with the young man and see how he was progressing.

Although he was still in the hospital and I could do nothing to help him, I felt a sense of comfort for as long as I knew that he was still hanging on to life. Part of me was still hurting and I felt in some way responsible for him. I was unable to sleep and continued to call the hospital throughout most nights to check on him. Finally, I called one morning and the nurse on duty informed me that he had expired. Oh my God, I felt so helpless and had no idea what I should do. I waited a few minutes and called back to the hospital, just to make sure that what I had just heard was correct. After all, maybe the person who answered before had made a mistake and given me the wrong information. With the second call, it was confirmed that the information was indeed correct and the young man had died.

I kept asking myself, "why did he run out in front of the car?"

Later finding out that he had a disability, I was hurting for the family and was mourning just as they were. I felt connected to them through the pain and was dealing with a great deal of grief. I was unable to sleep and had a loss of appetite. None of this was good for the baby that I was carrying. Thank Jesus for protecting my baby, because I had been dealing with a great deal of stress ever since I found out I was pregnant, and now this ordeal. I assured myself that this was going to be a strong baby.

After the death was confirmed, I began calling to find out which Funeral Home would be handling the funeral arrangements.

After many calls, I was able to locate his remains and found that there had been no funeral arrangements made.

I called the funeral home daily, only to find out that there were still no arrangements; the family was having trouble coming up with the funds to bury their son. Finally, after about two weeks, the family had been able to collect enough money to bury their son and he was officially buried. I could not erase the image, in my head, of the other young guys running off and leaving the young guy alone. This had proven to be a traumatic experience for me. No one really knew what I was going through daily. It was extremely hard for me to function normally and go on with my life without stressing over the fact that the young man's life had ended. It took me six months to gather my nerves and be able to drive again.

I would drive the same car in which I was driving when the horrible accident occurred, the same car into which the young man had run. I still think of him and don't believe I will ever forget him.

Chapter 3

TRUE COLORS

A few months had passed and we had decided to name the baby "London". I was now nine months pregnant with London and Hamilton had gone back to his old ways. I had been given a reprieve while dealing with the distress of the accident. We started arguing again and Hamilton accused me of messing up his car. I asked if he really felt that way and told him that his knowing how emotionally painful that accident had been for me made it all the more disappointing that he would even mention anything about it. I knew that his bringing this up was just his evil way of hurting me.

On his birthday, October 26, 1993, Hamilton picked me up from work. An argument ensued and we argued all the way from my job to my son, Andre's daycare. I was so angry that I told Hamilton not to worry about dropping me off at my sister, Michelle's house. I insisted that I would walk. That night, I fed and bathed Andre and got him ready for bed, took my shower and went to bed. I was unable to rest. There had been so much anger and frustration that day and I thought for sure that was the reason I was unable to go to sleep. The baby would not let me sleep and I did not know it at the time, but I was in labor. After much discomfort, pain, tossing and turning I told my sister that I didn't feel well. Around 2 am we called the hospital and told them we were on the way there. In the meantime, we kept calling Hamilton and could not reach him.

We arrived at the hospital and they checked me in and escorted me to my room. Michelle remained with me all morning. She called my job and informed my supervisor that I had been checked into the hospital and was in labor. We finally reached Hamilton on the phone and told him that I was in labor as well. When he finally arrived at the hospital, he reeked of alcohol and it was apparent that he had been out all night drinking. He was stinking drunk.

Hamilton stated that he couldn't stay in the room because he felt sick. I told him that he was going to stay in that room and see the birth of his daughter, London. He had not witnessed the birth of his first two daughters and I stressed the importance of him being there for the birth of London. He stayed and filled the room with the loud stench of alcohol. As the contractions got closer and closer, the hospital staff administered an epidural.

They got closer and closer and finally London's head was crowning.

Hamilton said he was about to pass out when he saw the head, but managed to hold it together. The doctor began instructing me to push, she was coming. Finally, there she was, my beautiful baby girl, my 8 pounds and 9 ounce daughter, London. We saw her for the first time and it hit Hamilton that he now has 3 daughters. He stayed around at the hospital and soon they moved me to a private room. He held the baby for a while and then stated that he was going to go home and get some sleep. He would then add a few finishing touches to the house so that when we left the hospital with the baby, we would go straight to his home and live with him.

We were released from the hospital three days later and Hamilton picked us up and took us home to the family house with him. His sister, Dorothy, had helped him get everything ready for us. Everything looked so beautiful. I was starting a new chapter in my life and felt confident that everything would be okay.

Hamilton took a week off from work to help me with the baby and my mother came over and spent some time to help out as well.

London was gorgeous and Andre was so happy to see his sweet baby sister.

Hamilton gave up smoking as a gift to his daughter and he didn't want anyone else smoking around his daughter either. Once he gave up smoking, he was able to smell the stale stench of old smoke in the house and it was making him sick.

He was then able to identify with what I was dealing with when they were all smoking around me and I was complaining about the smoke. He admitted that he had no idea that it smelled quite so bad.

After a week, Hamilton returned to work and my mother continued to come over and help me. He took Andre to school in the mornings and picked him up after work.

After about two weeks, I was able to get up and walk around the house much better. I had not only had a baby, but I had had a tubal ligation the day after the baby was born. After being home for 3 weeks, I asked my mother if she would keep London when I returned to work. I explained that she was a new born and I was uncomfortable leaving her with just anyone.

My mother originally said yes she would keep London and I asked her to let me know how much she would charge me to keep her. My mother waited until one week before I was to return to work and called me to say that she was not going to be able to keep London for me. When I inquired as to why she could not keep her, she said it was because I couldn't afford to pay her what she wanted. I was furious because I thought this was all settled and she waited until a week before I was to return to work to tell me something like this. Fortunately, I was able to find someone right across the street from my job to keep London. By the time six weeks came around I was tired of being in the house all day every day and was glad to return to work. Hamilton and I were getting along very well and I was glad to be going back to work and to church to be around my friends.

Chapter 4

CONFRONTATION

Once I got back in the groove of things, I was able to resume my daily routine of cooking and cleaning. I noticed that Hamilton had begun to come home later and later each day. Some days he would come in from work and then leave the house again, without any explanation. We had two vehicles at the house, a five speed truck and a car. One particular evening, Hamilton said he was going to shoot pool. I asked him if he would go by the store and pick up some pampers for London.

I explained that there was only one pamper left and he replied, "Will do."

He left and about 40 minutes later, London had messed in her pamper, so I changed her using the last pamper. Later she wet in her pamper and Hamilton had still not returned home with more pampers. There were no more pampers, so I used a pillow case to keep her dry. I was extremely upset that Hamilton had stayed out so long. He left around 6pm and he did not return home until 5am the next morning. He had taken the car and left the truck, which I was unable to drive, because it was a five speed.

When he finally returned, I greeted Hamilton with, "Where the hell have you been? Wherever you came from, you need to just go back there!"

This immediatcly started an argument. He slapped and shoved me and we followed suit with each of us calling the other out of their name.

I told him he was a low down bastard because he had stayed out all night and was a sorry excuse of a father for not bringing his baby some pampers after I stressed that she only had one left. I told him he could kiss me where the sun does not shine. He was obviously drunk and as usual I found women's names and phone numbers on small pieces of torn brown paper bags in his pockets. He was so intoxicated that he couldn't do anything but fall asleep. When he awoke, we picked up with the arguing exactly where we had left off.

I said "How dare you not think about your daughter's needs, you only think about your selfish behind!"

When mentioned he claimed that he had no idea whose names and numbers those were that I found in his pockets. I proceeded to tell him that if I catch him cheating, I will hurt him.

I then left for the store to get pampers for London. I hated arguing around my children and never wanted to put them in that type of situation. The next day, I told Hamilton we needed to talk about him staying out all night and coming in whenever he got ready. It was not fair to me nor his daughter. I told him that he acted like he did not give a damn about us. He asked me to lower my voice so that his kids would not hear us. We managed to have a peaceful discussion and come to some common understanding.

After a few months had passed, he surprised me with tickets to a concert. We went and had a wonderful time. Later, Hamilton had a seminar to attend for his job in Florida. We made special arrangements for the children and he took me with him. His sister kept London and Andre's father kept him.

We had a wonderful, stress-free, 4-day trip, leaving on Wednesday and returning on Sunday. Staying at a 5-Star Hotel at a wonderful resort, we spent some much needed quality time on the beach. Hamilton is almost like two different people at times and is a much better person to be around when he is not drinking. Before we left the resort to head home, Hamilton stated that he needed to pick up a friend in Pensacola named Mark who needed to ride back to Birmingham with us.

I said ok, not knowing this was an old friend that he used to hang out with who was "trouble".

Surprisingly, there were no problems during the ride home. It was a peaceful, uneventful ride. When we arrived back home, Hamilton's friend Mark came to the house. Mark lived up the street from us, with his mother and loved to party.

He always wanted Hamilton to go out and party with him, as if Hamilton did not have me and a newborn baby at home. It appeared that Hamilton forgot that he had me and a newborn baby at home as well, as he began to hang out with Mark more and more; coming in drunk as late as 3am and sometimes 4am in the morning.

I said "Hamilton, you are going to have to stop hanging with Mark so much."

His response was "Mark is sick, he had brain surgery."

I said "I don't give a damn! It hasn't stopped him from sleeping with every woman he sees, who will allow him to."

This behavior went on for about four months. Then I finally said "Either you stop hanging with Mark, or go live with him.

You are disrespecting me and the kids and I cannot continue to allow you to do this. You bring home the phone numbers of different women and only God knows what else you are doing. If you do not stop it, you can leave!"

He did not say anything else about it at the time; however I know he didn't like what I said. I had just had enough. I could not understand what made him think that it was alright for a married man to hang out all times of the night with a single man and a bunch of women.

Hamilton and I took the kids over to his sister's house one night and dropped them off. He said that he wanted the two of us to take a drive alone. We took a nice long drive. As we were riding on the freeway, I was looking out of the window at the cars driving by and out of nowhere, Hamilton slapped me across my head really hard.

I quickly turned to look at him and said "Why did you do that?"

He replied "You looking at your nigga?"

I said "What? I was looking at the cars go by on the freeway."

After we picked up the kids, went home and got them situated, I went down stairs to the den and slapped Hamilton as hard as I could.

I told him "Don't you ever hit me like that again. Are you crazy? You are a sorry bastard! I'm looking at the cars driving by going at a speed of 80 to 100 miles per hour and you are worried about me looking at a man? Seriously, you are sick!"

What was going on in his mind to make him think I could possibly be looking at a man, as fast as the cars were moving on the freeway? He was clearly making up his own scenarios in his head. He had not even been drinking when he did this.

The next day, Hamilton's friend came over and said they were going to shoot pool. Hamilton drove his truck. They had been gone about two hours, when I gathered the kids and put them in the car. I drove down the hill to the pool hall, just to see for myself exactly what was going on. I was going to start confronting him about his wrong doings. I parked the car right in front of the door and left the kids sitting in the back seat, assuring them that I would be right back. I walked in and spoke to the bartender while heading straight to the back. There were some gentlemen playing cards but no one was playing pool.

Who do I see sitting down at a table drinking with a woman? It was Hamilton. I walked hurriedly over to the table, catching him off guard.

I said "What is going on here? I know you not buying another woman drinks, when you have children at home."

The woman replied "He said he wasn't married."

I responded by asking "Was I talking to you?"

I then said "Hamilton, I know you not up in here buying drinks. I suggest you get up now!"

The woman's friend was sitting at another table and she said "Don't talk to my girlfriend like that!"

I quickly turned behind me and asked "Was I talking to you? I suggest you be quiet or we can take it outside. What would you like to do?"

The men held her back. I told them not to hold her back because she was going to learn to mind her business.

"But that's my friend" she said.

I said "Your friend seems to be a big girl, literally." I picked up both of the drinks off the table and, threw them on Hamilton and the woman with whom he was sitting.

I slapped him and said "Get your butt up and get to the car while you still can. Your children are waiting in the car."

I then looked back at the other woman and asked "Do you need to meet me outside? Next time, I suggest that you stop getting into other people's business when it does not concern you."

I knew I was causing a scene and I did not care. He had no right to be out there with those women while I was home with the children.

I got even more angry thinking about the fact that he had the nerve to slap me because he thought I was looking at a man and here he was out buying drinks for a woman. Hamilton inquired as to why I left the kids in the car and I answered with "the same way you were supposed to be shooting pool. So you buying drinks now? So this is what you do at the pool hall, go and meet women?"

He said "Why you have to come down here and act a fool? I wasn't trying anything with that woman; I was just talking to her and bought her a drink. I wasn't trying to sleep with her."

"Hamilton, you really think I'm dense. You can find fault in everyone but yourself. Listen to you, did what you just said make any sense to you? You get to hang out with your boys and do whatever you want while I stay home with the kids." I shouted.

Hamilton stayed home after the incident, although it didn't last long. A week later, he went out again and said he was going to shoot pool. This particular time he took the car and left the truck at home. He thought that because I could not drive a 5 speed, he would be safe leaving the truck. He was gone until almost midnight. Andre was gone for the weekend so I gathered London and the two of us got in the truck and I decided to give the 5 speed a try. It took a minute to get out of first gear but once I did it was smooth driving as long as I didn't have to come to a complete stop.

I arrived at my destination and found Hamilton talking to a lady and again, I approached him. When he saw me, I thought he was going to faint. He asked "What are you doing here?"

Without answering his question, I asked "How long are you planning to stay here? You have been gone to 'shoot pool' since 3pm today. I guess it got real good to you. I suggest you come home. You have done enough damage in one day, don't you think?"

The lady asked "Who is she Hamilton?"

I responded "His wife. Do I need to say anything more, slut?"

Hamilton barked, "Let's go!" He was so angry with me. He got in the car, knowing that I was in the truck, and sped off intentionally trying to leave me. I told London to hold on because her father was trying to play low down games. Instead of going home, he tried to out run me and disappear. Wherever he turned, so did I. Following as close as possible, so as not to get lost from him. He would go up the hill and so would I; however I didn't go fast because my child was in the truck and she and my own safety was most important. For some reason, I was able to drive that truck very well. Finally, after seeing that I was keeping up with him and he was unable to shake me, he went on home. Again I followed. I was so angry that he would give those women his time but would not give any to his daughter. I had a real problem with that. He did not like for me to embarrass him in front of anyone. He didn't show me any respect when he was with me and he didn't show me any respect when he was away from me. He told me that I wasn't crap. He proceeded to hit me across my head and I slapped him back.

He then took off his belt, grabbed me and threw me across the bed and beat me with that belt, while holding my head down in the bed with his knee on my bent arm. I was unable to get up, but as soon as I was able to break free from his grip, I got up and kicked him between his legs twice and did not regret it. I grabbed the belt as he was doubled over in pain and put it around his neck and tried to choke him with it.

I said to Hamilton "You are a menace to society. One day you will go to sleep and you may not wake up. If I were you, I would try to sleep with one eye open and one eye closed!"

The next morning, I got up and cooked breakfast, fed London, bathed her, took me a shower and got dressed for church. After Church, I came in and cooked dinner. Andre arrived home from his father's house and I got his school clothes ready for the upcoming week. I took some time to play with the children, and then I got dressed for bed and went to sleep.

Chapter 5

I Do

By the time London Was 10 ½ months old, she took her first steps. It was an exciting time and Hamilton and I were able to experience that together. This was a great family moment. She was potty trained at 11 months. She was growing up fast and I wanted her childhood to be peaceful and happy. I wanted the same for Andre. My desire was for them to grow up in a happy home with two parents who loved them. Children get their idea of how love looks and behaves when they are young and they grow up and sometimes mimic what they have seen. We all learn by watching. Was Hamilton showing Andre how a woman should be treated?

Was he showing London how she should expect a man to treat her? He did not even seem concerned about making me his wife. I wanted my children to respect the institution of marriage. These were definitely some things that I needed to think about. This was really not what I was focused on at that time. I just wanted Hamilton to be the man that I thought he was in the beginning. I wanted him to marry me, stop drinking so much and stop verbally and physically abusing me.

One evening my friends called and wanted me to join them to go out for happy hour. I asked Hamilton if he could watch the kids on Friday. He said sure. Well

Friday came and I started getting dressed. Hamilton asked "Where are you going?"

I replied "Did you forget? I told you I needed you to watch the kids this Friday so that I can go out with the girls."

He said "No, don't remember that. You cannot just spring these things on me at the last minute. In the future, you need to give me a two weeks' notice." So I didn't go. I elected to just stay home instead of arguing with him or trying to find someone else to watch the kids. I went to the hair salon that Saturday morning. When I got home Hamilton had been drinking and was ready to start a fight with me.

He met me at the door and said "Look at you! So you had to go and get all fixed up for your man. So who is he?"

Before I could even respond, he pulled me by my hair and said "You think you are so slick. Well I see you and you are not fooling me."

I said "Exactly what do you mean by that?" He grabbed me and started messing up my hair and said "It's too bad your man won't see you with your hair fixed this time. You just wasted your money!"

Then he slapped me really hard across my face. I hit him back and we began to fight. He threw beer in my hair, so I had to re-wash my hair and sit under the dryer. This was painful because every woman knows that it is no fun sitting under the hot dryer once, much less twice in one day. He was treating me like a dog. He said "Simone, you are going to keep playing around with me and I am going to kill you."

As much as I didn't want to, I really believed that he would seriously try to kill me. This was disturbing because I was really not doing anything. I had gotten my hair done, because it needed to be done. I was not even thinking about another man and just wanted him to change. He had become extremely jealous and this was very disturbing to know that he could be so jealous that he became delusional.

I was so miserable and kept wondering what I had done to deserve this type of treatment. I felt like every day was a fight for my life. When I got home daily, it felt as though I was stepping into the ring for a fighting match. My opponent, who unfairly happened to be the man who vowed to love me unconditionally, was always automatically bigger and stronger. Not only that, but he did not fight fair and always had an advantage.

The following week Hamilton kept the kids and I was able to go out with my girlfriends. It was much needed time out for me with the girls. This was one of the only times in which I was able to really relax and enjoy myself. When I was out with the girls no one was judging me, criticizing me, accusing me of looking at men and I did not feel as though I had to fight for my life. We had a wonderful night out and I made the most of it because I had no idea when I would be able to get out with them again. Not only that, but I had no idea what I would have to deal with when I returned home.

When I got home, at no surprise to me, Hamilton had friends over to the house and they had been drinking. The house reeked of alcohol and it was full of laughter and profanity. After they left, he came into the room and said "Simone, where did you go?"

I told him I had gone to happy hour as I stated before I left. He wanted to make love but I was not in the mood. It is hard to want to be intimate with a man when he abuses you more than he makes you feel loved. Of course he could never understand that. He was angry because I said no and he accused me of being with someone else while I was out. He told me I smelled like I had been having sex. I told him if you think so, whatever you say and I turned to walk away and get ready for bed. He grabbed my arm and pulled me back and slapped me hard across my head. As usual, I hit back and a fight ensued. We fought until we were both exhausted. When will this end I thought as I took a shower and went and slept in my son's room with my son. Once Hamilton got up to get ready for work, I returned to our bedroom and went back to sleep.

When I woke up, my face was red and swollen. I wondered how much longer we could continue this. I was tired of working so hard to cover my bruises. When Hamilton returned home, after work, we talked. I said "If we don't set a date to get married, I am leaving because I am not going to continue to live here and you don't marry me. I know it seems crazy to still want to marry a person who treats me like crap, but I loved Hamilton. I felt that somehow if we got married, he would realize how much I loved him and things would get better. The real fact of the matter is that changing your name or your marital status does not change your behavior. Hamilton needed to want to change in his heart and until he did, things would remain the same. This would have been a good time to exit the relationship rather than go deeper in.

Finally, Hamilton picked me up from work and to my surprise, he took me to the jewelry store and we picked out rings. We settled on a month and day. Hamilton then said that we wouldn't be able to get married that month and when I asked why he said because he was still married to his first wife.

I said "Your wife, what the hell do you mean? You told me you were divorced."

He said "Well I lied."

I yelled "You mean to tell me that I was pregnant and had a baby by you and you're still married? You made me look like a fool at your sister's wedding, walking around pregnant and you're still married. When in the hell were you planning to get a divorce?"

He said "I already filed."

I said "No wonder you can't marry me. You've been giving me the run around. Your whole family knew you were still married and couldn't tell me. What else have you lied to me about?"

He said that he knew if he had told me he would have lost me. It didn't make me feel any better that he chose to lie to me. Once he got a divorce, we still had to wait six months before we could be married. Once everything was finalized, we set a date. We decided to get married at the courthouse and not tell our families until afterwards. On the day that we chose to get married, I got off from work early and we went and got married. This was one of the happiest days of my life. The next day Hamilton sent me flowers on my job. Once we said "I do" things seemed to change for the worse.

Hamilton then said that he needed to set some much needed rules and boundaries for me to follow. He loved to drink liquor and had always had a problem handling the liquor. To make it worse, he liked to take a shot of liquor and chase it with a beer and then the abuse would begin. A month into the marriage, things got much worse. I should not have been surprised, but I had hoped that things would get better for us once we said "I Do". Hamilton began to get more possessive over me. He was more jealous and never wanted me to go anywhere.

Out of nowhere, I began to experience heavy bleeding, causing my menstrual cycles to be extremely heavy and last much longer than usual. This was a huge problem for me because I could not stand the smell of fresh blood. I was always very tired and felt drained. This continued for about 4 months and finally I called my Ob/Gyn and scheduled a check-up.

It was discovered that I had large fibroids and cysts. After some time had passed, I got a second opinion and it was confirmed that I had large fibroids and cysts and they needed to be removed as soon as possible. I would need to have a hysterectomy.

I waited until London was 14 months and decided to schedule my hysterectomy, which would have me down for about eight weeks. I contacted my support group which consisted of my mother and Dorothy and informed them that I was having surgery and would need help with the children. I also contacted Andre's father to solicit his assistance with helping to get Andre back and forth to school and helping to care for him while I was recovering and he agreed to help. Hamilton took off a week and a half from work for the surgery and to be there to help with London.

The surgery went well, but I had a high temperature and they had difficulty bringing it down. I remained in the hospital for seven days and was given lots of fluids. Once I got home, the recovery went well and the eight weeks went by really quickly. It was finally time to go back to work. I was feeling wonderful and managed to get back into the swing of things rather quickly. It was nice to be back on the job and around my co-workers. This gave me something other than home to focus on.

Upon my returning to work, Hamilton had a seminar to attend for work for several days in Ohio. He had some family in Ohio and he also had an ex-girlfriend whom lived there as well. He invited me to come along, however I didn't want to leave my kids and I had just returned to work after being out for eight weeks, so I didn't accompany him to the seminar.

Hamilton went alone and called me as soon as he arrived in Ohio to let me know that he arrived and that everything was going ok. Two days before his return, I called him in his hotel. He said he was getting ready for bed and that he would call me in the morning.

The next morning, I got the kids off to school and I went to work. After work I picked up the kids and accomplished the usual routine; I cooked dinner, fed them, bathed them and put them to bed. After the long day, I called Hamilton and we talked for just a minute. It felt as though he was rushing me to hang up the phone. He said that he would be returning home on the following evening and he was in the middle of packing his clothes and wanted to get to be early. For some reason, while Hamilton and I were on the phone, I felt he was with someone in his room. The background was very quiet.

There was no music playing and no sound of the television. The tone of his voice and the way that he was rushing me also said that someone was there. I did not press the issue, but instead I said goodnight and hung up the phone. This issue would have to wait until morning.

I called him the next morning and told him that I knew he had someone in the room the night before and I knew it was Betty.

He emphatically denied that anyone was there and I said "You are telling a damn lie! When you get your black butt home we are going to talk. I am so sick and tired of your mess. You didn't spend the night at your aunt's house and I know because I called and asked her."

He said that I made him so mad that he almost ran off the road. I told him good.

When he returned home the next evening, since he had a rental car, he took me to the casino that night. We argued but he did not want to hear what I had to say and had only taken me to the casino to serve as a distraction. Hamilton had to go to work that next morning which was a Saturday. After he had gone to work, the phone rang and I answered it. On the other end of the phone was a woman asking to speak to Simone.

I said "Speaking"

She said "When you called last night, Hamilton and I were making love."

If I could have gone through the phone, I would have. That is just how angry I was. My anger would not even allow me to hold my glass steady; I spilled juice in the answering machine and immediately called Hamilton to see what time he was getting off from work. I told him to come straight home from work and not make any stops. He kept asking me what was wrong and I maintained that I would talk with him when he got home. When he finally made it home, I met him with questions.

I asked "Exactly what did you do on your trip and who did you see?"

He said "Don't start with me, Simone. I didn't do anything!"

"Well someone named Betty called this morning and said otherwise. She said that when I called you, she was in your room and the two of you were making love. Now one of you is lying and my guess is that it is you!"

He replied "She is lying. I haven't even talked to Betty."

I said "You are lying! If you did not talk to Betty, then how did she know my name and how did she get our new telephone number?"

I pushed him and he pushed me back. He then started to choke me. I started hitting him in his head trying to make him release the grip around my neck. He would normally slap me in my head and face but this time he didn't.

He said "I will try not to hit you in your face because I don't want to mess up your beautiful face. I will hit you where no one will see." I guess he somehow thought choking me was a better option. I could wear turtle necks or scarves to cover. He began hitting me in my back, stomach and other covered areas. This fight went on for some time and then we both relinquished.

Another sad thing about our situation is that the fighting never solves anything. Once he chokes me and I break free, we continue to serve hits and punches, pushing, shoving and yelling until we get tired and go to bed. The initial issue is still there, and nothing has changed. That particular fight did not change the fact that he lied about being with Betty and he never admitted that he was lying. After fighting for nothing, we always get up the next morning as if nothing had happened and I have the pleasure of working to cover my bruises.

A week later, I began to get really sick. My stomach was hurting badly and I had a discharge, so I had a co-worker in the lab to check my urine. After checking, she told me that I had better call my Ob/Gyn. So I made an appointment and Hamilton accompanied me to the visit.

I gave the doctor all of my symptoms and after examining me, he told me to get dressed and meet him in his office. When I entered the office, he placed a call to the front desk and asked the attendant to send Hamilton to the office as well. He talked to the both of us and told Hamilton that he needed to make a decision about our marriage. He gave me enough medicine for the both of us. I was absolutely Furious! I could not even trust him to go out of town without me. Now his being unfaithful was endangering my health. We got the prescription filled and when we got home I cursed him out. He maintained that he did not do anything. I told him to just stop lying before I make him go to his own doctor and get his own medicine. This led to more arguing and he pushed me. I pushed him back. He had the nerve to accuse me of being with someone else.

I yelled "How dare you try to put that lie off on me! You're as dense as I thought you were!"

We began to fight. He was choking me and I was hitting him in his head. Then I kicked him between his legs and finally he released his hands from around my neck and left the room. I was so angry it was hard to think straight. I was sick and tired of his mess. He had the nerve to do wrong, get caught, lie about it and then accuse me of being with someone else. He was treading on thin ice with me. I was in the closet trying to get my clothes and calm down when I stumbled upon his gun. All I could think of was hurting him the way that he had hurt me. I grabbed the gun and checked for bullets. I will show him, I thought. I was contemplating putting it back, when I heard Hamilton coming into the room, yelling and cursing at me.

He stormed into the closet and I turned and pointed the gun at him in a quick moment of rage. In that moment, I thought I had taken all that I was going to take from him.

He said "What the hell are you doing, Simone? Put that down!"

As I walked toward him with the gun and a crazed look of anger on my face, he saw that I was serious about shooting him. He had a look of fear on his face and turned and started running up the stairs. I shot at him and the bullet just missed him. I shot again. If he had hesitated for a split second, he would have been hit. I did not see him again that night. He knew that he needed to stay away from me until I calmed down. I went into the bathroom and just cried before taking a shower and going to bed.

I thought about what I had done and was almost afraid when I realized that I could have killed him that night. I should not have let him send me into such a rage of anger. After all, I had children and I had to think of how this all would have affected them. If I had killed him, I could have gone to jail and my children would have been left without either one of us. I needed to consider finding a way of escape. This situation had gone too far and someone was going to get seriously hurt or worse, die!

The next morning, I went to get my hair done as if nothing had happened. I had forgotten about the bruises on my neck from being choked the night before, until my beautician began to wash my hair and said "Simone, who choked you?"

Immediately, I said "Hamilton and I were playing around. He made a mistake and put his hand around my neck. We were just playing."

She looked at me, for what seemed like an hour, and said "Are you sure that is what happened, Simone?" I lied and said "Yes, that is what happened."

I quickly changed the subject and she continued to look at me and followed my direction of the new subject. I felt as if I was under a spell of some sort. How could I continue to defend him? I wanted to scream out for help and yet I said nothing and I continued to defend him. I knew what he was doing to me was not right, but I remained in the home subjecting myself to the abuse. My kids were affected negatively as well.

Every time Hamilton would do something wrong, he would follow it the next day by sending roses to my job in an effort to make up for what he had done. He sent so many flowers, that I started asking who they were from. My co-workers would always say that they were from my husband. It got to the point that I really did not even want the flowers. I wanted to give them back to the person delivering with a note that said "Return to Sender". Or better yet, take them home and tell Hamilton to shove them where the sun does not shine. I allowed this abuse to happen and continue because I was too afraid to leave.

His sister, Dorothy, would come by our house when she got off from work about every other evening. One particular evening, she got dropped off at our house and she asked me to drop her off at home. I said sure and the next thing I knew, Hamilton was taking her home.

Well I went over to Dorothy's house and asked her why she didn't want me to take her home. She stated that Hamilton said he would take her. I told her and Hamilton they were up to no good. Hamilton got mad because I told him he would jump for her. Nothing Dorothy ever did was wrong in his eyes and he was always there to defend her. She was also always defending him. I knew that she knew how badly her brother was treating me and she never said anything to me at all about it. He shoved me and I shoved his butt back. We started fighting, serving it up to each other as if we were playing a competitive game of tennis; he hit then I hit. He slapped me and I slapped him back. He called me a witch and I told him if you never called your mother one, what gives you the right to call me one. I told Dorothy that this was all her fault. He pushed me into the closet and grabbed me by the hair. I kicked him and tried to pull his eyes out.

I couldn't let him think he could just beat on me and I wouldn't fight him back. This was one of the worst fights ever and Dorothy and her husband were having a difficult time trying to break us up. Her husband got on the phone and called Hamilton's brother out of Tennessee to tell him what was going on. He was asking to speak to Hamilton but that was definitely not going to happen as we were both caught up in the heat of anger and we were quite irrational.

Dorothy yelled "Hamilton let her go right now!" He let me go and started to walk off. Then that bastard took a cheap shot; he came back real quick and slapped me in my face. I lunged after him. He ran over and grabbed London. I ran to take her from him, but he wouldn't give her to me. He was taking it to another level when he grabbed my baby.

He should never have put her in the middle. It was bad enough that she had to see her mother and father fighting, but he made it worse when he grabbed her and ran. What was he planning to do with her? I was livid and was not sure what I would do when I got my hands on him. I believe Dorothy could see that he had really sparked something in me.

She kept screaming "Hamilton, give her the baby!" I got my baby and left the house immediately. I just drove around for a while crying profusely. Finally, I went home. About 30 minutes after I arrived home, Hamilton came in. His brother, Roosevelt, called and I didn't feel like talking. He explained that he only wanted to make sure I was okay. I bathed London, fed her and then I took a shower and went to bed. Again, like clockwork the cycle continued.

We got up the next morning as if nothing had happened the night before. Someway, somehow the vicious cycle had to end. I got up and went to the beauty shop to get my hair done. Hamilton stayed home and London stayed with him. I got to the beauty shop and sat for about 20 minutes before Tricia called me back to perm my hair. We talked for a while, she asked how the kids were doing and I told her they were wonderful. Finally, Tricia started washing the perm out of my hair. I forgot about the bruises around my neck and she asked about them again. Again, I lied so she finally left it alone.

Chapter 6

LIFE CHANGING EVENTS

Whenever I did get up enough nerve to leave, I packed a few things and went to stay at my sister's house for a few days. He called me and sweet talked me into coming back home. The kids and I would end up back at home, against my better judgement. I knew I should not have gone back, but I just did not know what else to do. It was as if the craziness, the fighting and the abuse were my normal and in some ways I had allowed myself to become comfortable with that because it was what I knew. I didn't like it and I wanted it to end, but somehow I felt I was stuck and had no other options. I had lost my drive and no longer saw the value in myself.

A week after I returned home, I went over to my girlfriend's house and hung out over there for a while. There was nothing major happening, we were just kicking it. I wasn't there long, but when I got home Hamilton asked me where I was. I told him I had been over at a friend's house.

He said "I called and she said you were never over there, so where did you go?"

I said "When I left my friend's house, I stopped at the store to buy some gum and then I came straight home."

He looked at me with disgust as if he did not believe me and I knew this was not the end of it. However if he didn't push the issue, I was certainly not going to. Besides, I did not feel like fighting anyway. I just wanted to go to bed and go to sleep.

When I woke up the next morning, Hamilton came to me and asked me for some gum. I knew there was something to this because we just woke up and he was asking me for a piece of gum. I was thinking, go and brush your teeth, but I gave him a piece of gum.

He said "Where did you buy this gum?"

I said "At the store, down the hill."

Hamilton left the house and I had no idea where he was going. He went to the store and called me back to inform me that the gentleman at the store said they don't carry that kind of gum. I asked Hamilton what service station he went to and he said "Down the hill."

I said "Well Hamilton there were about five service stations down the hill from our house. They don't all carry the same brand or type of items. I cannot believe you are checking up on me!"

It didn't hit me until later that Hamilton didn't even chew gum. He went through all of that trouble to check and see if I really went to the store and bought gum last night. He also called my girlfriend and she was very upset.

I asked her what he said. She told me that my husband asked her if I was over there. He got very angry with her because she said "If you can't keep up with your own wife, how the hell do you think I can? Hear me clearly Hamilton, don't call my house again!"

She hung up the phone. When we got home from work, we started arguing. I said "I need to know why you felt the need to call my girlfriend to see if I was at her house last night. Also why would you go to the service station to see if I bought gum? You have trust issues and I am a grown woman!"

He clearly did not trust me because he was doing so much dirt himself. At that moment, I knew he had some serious issues. He was terribly insecure and he had been subjecting me to his insecurities. He was afraid and fearful, not to mention jealous. Undoubtedly, he did not feel that he was enough to keep me. He was always accusing me of looking at or wanting to be with other men. He abused me and tried to make me afraid of him, in order to control me.

When I stated that I was a grown woman, he grabbed me and slapped me across my mouth. We started fighting and he told me that he would kill me. He shoved me out of the way, went and got his gun and pointed it at me. I ran out the back door, ran to the neighbor's house and told them to call the police. I explained that Hamilton had a gun and was threatening to kill me.

This is the subdivision that Hamilton grew up in, so all of the neighbors knew him and his family. I had run out of the house in such a rush, without any shoes and I was barely dressed. I did not go back home until the police went over with me. The police went in and surveyed the home. They spoke to me for a short period and questioned me as to what happened. I told them that Hamilton had started a fight, choked me and had then pulled his gun on me and threatened to kill me. They proceeded to arrest Hamilton.

His sister, Dorothy came over and she wasn't worried about me at all. She was only concerned about Hamilton. She said "Don't take his car. You know how crazy he is about his car."

I called my mother and she came and picked up London and me. I still did not tell my mother all that had been going on.

I just made it look as though that night was an isolated incident. Fortunately, Andre was over at his father's house. Hamilton was released from jail on Saturday. Although he was released, I continued to stay at my mother's house. I knew I would soon have to make a permanent decision about my future. After a week had passed, I went back home to Hamilton and we sat down to talk.

I said "Hamilton, maybe we need to buy our own house and get out of your family's house. I'm thinking this will make our marriage better." I was still not ready to accept that he was who he was. I acted as if I had no clue that life changing events were not going to change our relationship for the better. Actually, each event had made it worse. First, I thought things would change for the better once our baby, London was born. I was wrong, it did not.

Next, I thought the two of us moving forward with getting married would make the abuse stop. I was wrong again. We set a date and got married and things got worse. They were both life changing events and they did not accomplish what I wanted them to accomplish. Then, there I was suggesting that we move out of the family home and purchase our own home. I was getting deeper and deeper invested with him and was fooling myself into thinking that buying a new home would help. I was making another desperate attempt to change our relationship with a life changing event.

We started driving around looking at houses without any assistance from an agent. We took the next step and went to the bank and got approved for a loan. After we were approved for a loan and knew exactly how much house we qualified for, we found a realtor to help us in our search.

We discussed our price range and started looking in different areas for our new home. After about six months of looking, we finally found a house that we loved. We dropped in on an open house and decided it was going to be our home. We put a contract on the house and 30 days later, we closed on our new home. I thought that buying a new house of our own would change things for the better, but things got worse after 3 months of living in our own home.

Hamilton and I fought constantly. Our neighbors probably thought the police lived there; they were called out to the house so many times. The police recognized us when they saw us out in the neighborhood. This was so embarrassing. Apparently it was not embarrassing enough to cause me to leave.

Hamilton went to the grocery store one evening and they had people sitting outside signing, those interested, up for home alarm systems. Hamilton felt that we could use an alarm system for our new house, so he purchased the system. Shortly thereafter, the motor went out in the car. We could not get the car fixed right away so Hamilton and I began to ride to work together, until we were able to get the car repaired.

One particular day we returned home from work, we pulled into the driveway and into the garage and we noticed that the door going into the house was wide open. I instantly felt something. Hamilton and I looked at each other because we knew we had closed the door when we left for work that morning.

As we entered the house, Hamilton said "Wait down here and let me check upstairs." He went up and looked around for a few minutes.

There was a chilling silence until he hollered down the stairs to me stating that someone had broken into the house and we had been robbed. We began to look around carefully making sure that the perpetrators were not still in the house. Upstairs they had kicked in our back door, off from the deck. We looked around, touching nothing and then called the police.

Once the police arrived he told us that six other houses were broken into the same way, within the week. They had all been in our area. Hamilton told the police that we had just purchased a security system at the store and he believed that they were the ones who found out which houses didn't have security systems and broke in. He called the grocery store to let them know there were people setting up outside their store and then robbing homes.

Once we received our police report, we called the insurance company. They came out to survey the damage and requested a list of our stolen items. We submitted the list along with our police report. I was instantly afraid of sleeping in my house because the back door was not secure. There was a great deal of uncertainty, not knowing if the robbers would return. I felt violated and insecure. There was an eerie feeling that they could have done something to our food, so we did not take any chances. We threw away all the food out of the refrigerator and anything that came in a package out of the pantry. I cleaned the house from top to bottom. What if they bugged the house? What if they hid cameras around the house, and now they were watching us? I had to get a grip and control my thoughts. I did not feel safe with Hamilton because of the abuse and now I felt even less safe after the break in.

Over the weekend, Hamilton had some cousins come in for the football game and they came by to visit. Hamilton left with them and they all went over to his sister and brother in law's house. I asked him how long he would be gone.

I said "Please don't be gone too long. You know I'm scared in this house by myself. We never knew when or if the robbers would come back to pay us a second visit. After a couple of hours had gone by and Hamilton had still not returned, I took London and we went over to his sister's house. When I got there more of his family had arrived. They had asked about me and wanted to meet me, but Hamilton told them that I was busy. He was shocked that I was there. He asked why I left the house open and I told him the same reason he had left the house open and he didn't want to come home.

I met some of the family members that I had never seen before and they were all glad to finally meet London and me. By the time we left Dorothy's house, Hamilton was drunk and when we arrived home he definitely wanted to argue. He was angry that I had shown up at his sister's house.

He told me that I should have stayed home and I said "Why should I have stayed home? You didn't stay home. You showed no concern about us. A real man would not have left us here in this house knowing that it was not secure and I was afraid. Wherever you smell liquor you run to it!"

He slapped me and pushed me to the floor and told me not to talk to him that way. As he was walking away, I stuck my foot out and attempted to make him fall.

Then, while he was off balance, I grabbed his leg from behind him. He fell flat on his face and I jumped on his back and began to choke him from behind.

I angrily said "Talk bad now!" I proceeded to put my knee in his back to let him see how it feels when the shoe is on the other foot. He has had me in that position so many times that I lost count. I didn't like it and used that moment as an opportunity to show him how it felt. I am not sure that it made a difference to him at all.

"It doesn't feel good does it?" I asked.

Without giving him a chance to answer, I slapped him in the back of the head and kept pushing my knee in his back. He said "Simone, when I get up I'm going to beat you!" And I said "when you get up?" I used every ounce of strength in my body to hold him in that uncomfortable position, but he was so drunk and exhausted, he fell asleep. I didn't want him to go to sleep. I wanted him to stay awake and feel the pain that I was trying to inflict. Finally, there was no use in tiring myself out because he had fallen asleep. I left him lying right there on the floor, went to take a shower and went to bed.

The next morning, as if nothing had happened the night before, London and I left early and went shopping. It was a great way to get out of the house. Hamilton was still on the floor. We stayed out shopping until late, we had lunch and then we stopped by one of my girlfriend's house to visit. We enjoyed our day. By the time we got home, Hamilton was downstairs shooting pool. London and I got ready for bed. She fell asleep and I decided I would watch some TV. I was staring at the screen, but merely trying to relax and unwind.

Hamilton came upstairs and to my surprise, he had not been drinking.

He said "Simone I want to talk to you. I know I haven't been a very good husband to you and I blame myself for that. Regardless as to how I treat you, you continue to take care of me. You take such good care of the house and these kids. I know I drink a little too much, but I do love you girl. You just seem to know how to strike all the nerves that make me so angry."

I replied "Oh really?"

He said "Let's take the kids and go on a family trip to the Aquarium. We can rent a townhouse near Roosevelt and they can come by and we can cook and have a great time."

I said "That sounds good Hamilton." This was another attempt to hold onto the false hope that an event will make our relationship better.

This time it was all Hamilton's idea and not mine, however I still grabbed a hold of the hope. It sounded like a good idea. We booked a trip for three days. We took his two girls, London and Andre and we had a marvelous time. Having never all taken a trip together, we left on Thursday evening and went to the Aquarium on Friday. On Saturday Roosevelt and his wife came by. We cooked dinner, played cards and had a great time together. Even the kids expressed that they had a great time. When we returned home from the trip we had a great work week. I felt pretty good about the way things were going, although we had had good weeks before and then all hell seemed to break loose. I remained positive and hopeful that this trip would mark a turnaround for our marriage.

Chapter 7

MANAGING TIME

My girlfriend Fran's niece was getting married and Fran gave her a bachelorette party. I went to help with the decorations and get things set up. Everything looked so beautiful. The bride-to-be was so happy that she was glowing. She was going to make a beautiful bride and I wished her much peace and happiness in her marriage.

Although I was in an abusive relationship, I still wanted to see other couples do well and be happy together. We had a great evening and the party went very well. My aunt was at my house staying the night, so I made sure to get in early so I could spend some time with her. When I arrived home, Hamilton had some of his friends over and everyone was out on the deck. It was a nice evening to be outside and he had grilled some food.

I joined them on the deck and we were all talking when Hamilton told me to go in the house. I told him I wasn't ready to go in and he said I told you to get inside.

"I'm talking to your brother!" I said. I looked at my aunt and hesitantly got up and went inside. My aunt followed me into the kitchen and we were in there talking. Shortly thereafter Hamilton's friend came inside and asked if he could talk to me about something.

I said "Yes, sure." He wanted to know if we would mind watching his daughter for a few days; He wanted to surprise his wife with a trip for their anniversary. I said of course and told him that sounds very romantic and I thought it would be a great idea.

Hamilton walked in and wanted to know what was going on and I said nothing. He would not drop it so I told him that his friend wanted us to keep the baby while he surprised his wife for their honeymoon.

Hamilton told his friend that he needed to get back outside and I asked him what was wrong with him. Here was clearly jealous of me talking to his friend at all. I was outside and he forced me to go inside and now that I am inside, he comes in to see what I am doing and is still not satisfied. There was clearly no pleasing him. I went outside to get a few wings off the grill and asked Hamilton what was the problem. We stood right inside the door talking while my aunt was right there in the kitchen.

He said "Simone, get your butt in the house NOW!"

I said "Stop telling me what to do!" At that moment, he opened the storm door and pushed me inside. The door caught the heel of my right foot causing me to fall to the floor. I yelled out and my aunt ran into the family room asking what was going on.

My foot was hurting badly and I looked down and saw that it was also bleeding.

I said "Auntie, I'll tell you what's going on; he is going to jail for acting like a fool!" I had not been able to talk to anyone about Hamilton. I called 911 and the police came and took him to jail. Of all the people he could have called to get him out of jail, he called my aunt. What hurt the most was that she actually went and got him out.

I was furious and I asked her "How could you get him out of jail? I am your niece. Did you forget why the police were called to come and take him to jail? You were here and you heard all of the commotion. You saw what he did to my foot. Perhaps you should take him back to Georgia to your house." She did not seem to feel bad about getting him out of jail and instead made me feel as though I was overreacting.

As the weekend came to a close, I was retracing all that had happened. The weekends are always horrible and Monday through Friday always goes by really fast. There we were beginning another work week.

"Lord please slow the week down and give me some peace."

My only reprieve was doing something that I really loved to do. I was active on the usher board at my church and when my pastor went out to preach he would take us along to usher. Our usher board would often get together for activities with each other. We would normally either meet at a member's home, at a restaurant or at the church. One particular weekend all of the ushers were invited to one of the member's home. Hamilton did not want to come with me so he said he would stay home and watch the kids.

I gave him a phone number where I would be just in case there was an emergency and he needed to reach me. We had dinner and played games. The host insisted that I take my husband a plate home for dinner. It was great to get together and have some fun as a group, outside of the church. We started to wrap up the games and everyone began leaving the gathering.

I left and was heading home when I thought I saw Hamilton approaching; he was coming up the hill in a black truck. I did not see the kids in the vehicle with him, so I rushed into our driveway and pulled into the garage. As I got out of the car I asked Hamilton where was he going? I went up the steps holding the plate that I had brought home for him. Once I got to the kitchen, Hamilton was right behind me. I turned and he startled me.

He said "Where the hell have you been?"

I said "You know I went over to my church member's house. I gave you the phone number.

"Where were you Hamilton and why did you leave the kids at home by themselves?" I put the plate down on the table and Hamilton charged me from behind. I fell to the floor and quickly tried to roll over and get up. He kicked me very hard in my stomach and then slapped me. He started dragging me across the kitchen floor.

He said "I called that number and someone told me that you were not there."

I said "They probably told you that because I had already left."

He said "No, you know your butt was never there." There I was lying on the floor hurting so badly I could hardly move. He left me lying there all alone in pain for quite a while.

After about an hour, he finally came back and said "Get your butt off the floor."

When I was finally able to get up, my stomach was in so much pain and one side of my face was very sore and swollen. My lip was bleeding and I had a large bruise on my arm. I would surely have to work to cover these bruises as I always did before going out in public.

I didn't have a vehicle when I initially met Hamilton so he used this to his advantage. I was 12 years younger than Hamilton and he used the car as one of his many attempts to control me. He would disconnect the car so I couldn't go anywhere. He monitored what I did, where I went and how long I stayed. I could not even run errands for the house without the pressure of being scrutinized. When I went to the grocery store I had to be back by a certain time.

He took the time to go over the grocery list with me and then tell me how long I had to get the groceries and get back to the house. I was so terrified of being late, that I would run around the grocery store with my buggy keeping a close eye on my watch. Constantly checking the time, I was trying to make it back home on time.

There was no room for error. I was always hoping there was no line in the grocery store, or I didn't run into anyone in the store that I knew and wanted to stop and talk with, no extra traffic on the road and no other uncontrollable situations. There was no extra time allotted for the unexpected. I stopped communicating with my mother for about a year because I didn't want her to know how bad Hamilton was treating me. It was not hard to go that long without dealing with my mom because she never wanted to watch the kids.

Whenever Hamilton and I wanted to go out to a movie, dinner or a concert she would always tell me she was busy.

When my girlfriend called, we would talk on the phone for hours laughing and taking trips down memory lane. She and I worked together and we never got together outside of work anymore. One day I got sick at work and they took me downstairs to the clinic. I fell out while in the clinic. I was so stressed out and was harboring so many secrets that it was starting to affect my health. They called my husband and began to run a lot of tests. Saying that I needed some rest and relaxation, they sent me home.

A week later Hamilton and I went to a gospel concert to see Donnie McClurkin, Yolanda Adams, Fred Hammond and Kirk Franklin.

The gospel music was so soothing to my spirit and brought me a sense of peace. I closed my eyes, sang along and became so full! The concert was fabulous and I really enjoyed it. I needed a night of gospel music and was filled with the spirit.

The next morning I went to church and I was still full knowing what I had gone through a week before with Hamilton. I was never one to shout in church. I had always felt the presence of God and gotten full but had never shouted before. We had a rather large congregation and I guess the Lord wanted my testimony to be shared on that particular Sunday. The choir was singing the song "I almost let go but God's mercy kept me" by Kurt Carr. When the song ended I had made it up on my feet and was clapping, singing and crying. I began to shout and the whole congregation got quiet.

I spoke and said "Nobody knows what I've been going through but I stand here today to tell you that it has been rough for me. God turned me around and placed my feet on solid ground. I may be smiling on the outside but you don't know the hurt and shame I feel on the inside."

I just kept speaking and thinking about all the abuse I've been going through. The usher came and got me and walked me outside of the sanctuary. I gathered myself and then I went back inside.

The Pastor said "You know you just don't know what a person is going through and how they are hurting sometimes. You also never know how the Lord is going to use you. The Lord touches everyone differently."

The pastor was shocked and said he had never seen me like that before. I got happy all over again and I was still very full when I got home.

My mother called me and said she got a phone call from a church member and they had told her that I got happy in church today. She asked me if I was alright and I said yes. I thought it was very odd that someone would call my mother and tell her what happened at church, before I could even get home to tell her myself. I then took a shower and went to bed. I no longer remembered anything that happened, until later that night. As I slept the Lord let me recite it all over again. I heard myself crying in my sleep and Hamilton woke me up. It was just about time to get ready for work anyway. When I got up, I never really opened my eyes. I was crying as I was walking to the bathroom and I was still crying in the shower. Hamilton appeared to be frightened because he had never seen me this way. He kept asking me what was wrong and I just kept telling him that God is good.

I spent the whole week full of God's grace and his love for me.

The very next weekend Hamilton's brother Roosevelt and his wife came to town to visit. Whenever they came, it was always a lot of heavy drinking going on. I made it a point to pull Roosevelt to the side and tell him if he didn't mind please try not to drink so much. I explained that when Hamilton drinks a lot he becomes violent and starts arguing with me and he always ends up starting a fight with me. When we first moved into our new house, we had a major fight and Hamilton put a hole in the wall in the hallway. He attempted to cover the hole up with a plaque so that the family would not see it when they came to visit. Roosevelt and his wife stayed at his sister's house while they were visiting. Just as I expected, Hamilton came in and started a fight as soon as he got home.

He wanted to fight for no real reason other than because he couldn't handle his liquor. He flipped all the lights on, came into the bedroom and snatched the covers off me in the middle of the night. He told me to get my butt up and fix him something to eat. I asked him why he was waking me up at 2am in the morning. He shouted again for me to get up and fix him something to eat. I told him that I would not get up and cook him anything to eat and I suggested that he either go to bed or warm him up something from the refrigerator. I reiterated that I was not cooking. He grabbed me by my arm and pulled me out of the bed onto the floor telling me I won't be going to sleep this night. This caused a big fight. I did not have to do very much this time. I basically just held him off of me and tired him out. As usual, he was so drunk that we fought until he passed out.

I got back into the bed and went to sleep. I was so tired

of this and knew something had to change and soon.

Chapter 8

Leave My Mommy Alone

The following week I wanted to go out with the girls and Hamilton did not want to watch the kids. I really needed to go out with my girlfriends so I did not allow his unwillingness to keep the kids to stop me. I asked my girlfriend's aunt, Bertha, to watch the kids. Bertha agreed to watch the kids and the two of us became very close and she became a listening ear. We could talk about anything. As time progressed, Hamilton began to be really mean and take his feelings for me out on London. I never understood how he could do that. She was an innocent child, his child, which had nothing to do with our problems. This clearly meant nothing to him because he had no problem mistreating her and verbally abusing her.

When she would cry her dad would say to her, "Go back over there to your mom. I don't have any kids. Mama's babies Papa's maybe."

This made London cry even harder. Every time Hamilton got upset with me, he would tell London she was not his. He would repeatedly tell me to get my butt out of his house and I would tell him I would in due time. The truth was, a part of me was afraid of staying with him and the other part was afraid of leaving him. Every time we got into a fight, I would call the police and he would get taken to jail. The police would ask if I wanted to press charges and each and every time I would say no. I knew that Hamilton worked around kids and I didn't want him to lose his job.

My mother finally began to say "why don't you just leave him?"

But I could not leave just because others felt that I should. I told my mother "I have to leave when I am ready and only then will I be strong enough to leave." I was convinced that I could not leave. I was afraid to leave because I felt that I couldn't make it by myself with two children. Hamilton had managed to make me doubt myself and I was no longer sure of the greatness that I knew I had inside of me. I believed any of the lies that he had told me about myself. His ugly words spoken to me had planted seeds of doubt in my mind and they were growing like wildflowers.

One night Hamilton and I were arguing and fussing at each other and it got much louder than usual. Every time I lay down, he would pull the covers off of me and refuse to allow me to go to sleep.

I was yelling for him to stop. They normally did not, but this particular night the kids got out of bed.

London came into the room and said "Daddy, daddy stop fighting mommy."

Hamilton said "Your momma is crazy baby." I just sat there as if I was immobilized by the fear of what I thought could happen next. Even Andre took on the role of trying to protect his mom. I was proud of him for trying, but did not want him to get hurt. He ran into the room with his little fist up ready to fight Hamilton. His little fist was clenched tightly and his face was distorted with anger.

Hamilton said "Andre, what you gone do little nigga?"

I told Hamilton "If you touch him, you will die tonight!" I meant those words with all of my being.

I jumped up from the bed and took the kids back to bed and stayed with each of them until they calmed down and fell asleep. This had never happened before and the fear of what could have happened really had me upset. I know that this was not the first time that they have ever heard us fighting and I was overwhelmed with the emotions of what they must have felt all of the other nights lying in their beds full of fear as we fought. I always thought that Hamilton would never physically hurt the kids, but there was also a time that I thought he would never physically hurt me either. I could not risk him ever hurting our kids. I believe this is the night that opened my eyes. I really saw that it was time to get my kids and go! I could no longer stay in this situation, because he was not just hurting me physically but he was really hurting me emotionally as well.

He may not have hit our kids or hurt them physically, but he was hurting our kids emotionally as well. London began to wet the bed every night because she was nervous that her father and I would fight. They were no longer those happy kids. London cried more than she laughed. How was it that I did not see what was happening to them for so long? I was so consumed with the pain I was feeling that I let my kids down. All of the red flags and flashing neon lights were there. I had just chosen to overlook them because I wanted my marriage to work out.

I asked God "Lord if I take one step, will you do the rest?" I prayed all day every day. I began to really consider an exit strategy. I started driving around looking for reasonable apartments on my lunch break. I knew in my heart I had to change my current situation as quickly as possible.

I treated it as if it was a matter of life and death. No more hoping, wishing and reaching out into the dark for a change. It was amazing that I was not willing to make the change for me, but when I realized the impact it was having on my children, change became necessary.

One day one of my co-workers overheard me talking on the phone and when I hung up she said "Ms. I wasn't trying to listen to your conversation, but I overheard you talking. I would never have known that you were going through anything. You're always smiling and happy."

I replied "that is because I know how to hide what I am feeling."

She asked me where I was looking for apartments and gave me a few suggestions of places in which I should look. One day, I returned to the office from my lunch break.

I had used my break to go out looking at apartments. My other co-worker said "Simone, Hamilton called and left a message that your daughter, London, had an accident at the school and was rushed to the hospital. I did not panic, but instead I called the school and asked to speak to the director. I told her who I was and that I was trying to see what had happened to London. I explained that her father had left a message on my job that London had been involved in an accident at the school and had to be rushed to the hospital. The director placed me on hold and when she returned to the phone, she had London with her.

The director woke London from her nap and said "See, your daughter is alright. You were informed incorrectly."

She then allowed me to speak with London. I told her that I would like to have a conference with her when I got off that evening and she said sure. I got to the school that evening and we sat and talked. I told her what was going on at home. She said she knew something was going on because of the information that she had been given. She had also noticed that London's countenance had changed and she had not been that same happy child lately. The director said she woke London up so my mind would be at ease. I told her I really appreciated it. I told her I was in the process of moving into my own place and I would let her know as soon as I had secured a place and moved. I also explained that once that happens no one will be allowed to pick up London except me, unless I instruct otherwise. She said that she understood and the school would follow my instructions.

I shared with her that I've been in a place that was really dark and that there have been so many times that I wanted to take my life. Looking at my kids every day is what kept me from killing myself.

My heavenly father has been so good to me. I've had to go to work with a black eye, sometimes two. He told me that he would stop hitting me in the face. I would rather he not hit me at all, but I was relieved that he stopped hitting me in my face. It was much harder to hide bruises on my face. I've had handprints around my throat and bruises on my body. I almost gave up many times. The devil thought he had me but Jesus came and grabbed me. God's mercy kept me so I wouldn't let go.

Thank you Lord Jesus! I realize when you are a child of God you must say that no matter what the circumstances are or what you see, you must still trust God.

I was in an abusive relationship with Hamilton that was kept hidden for many years. Some suspected that I was being abused, but because I would not admit it, nothing was ever done about it. If it had not been for the Lord and knowing my kids needed me I don't know where I'd be right now.

Have you ever hurt so bad on the inside it seemed like your insides were melting away? But the outside was just a shell that people could see while trying to keep a smile on your face. That was me; I kept my unspoken truth hidden at all times. It was hard, especially considering how I wanted to kill myself every day. I thought about it often and then felt guilty thinking, as a child of God, suicide should not have crossed my mind. I felt so alone and depressed. I knew my father God had me but the life I was living with this man was taking all of my strength and sanity.

Thank God for Jesus that I started growing stronger again. I was finally beginning to get my power back.

Chapter 9

STEPPING OUT ON FAITH

The motor was going out slowly in the car. Hamilton knew I had no way of getting around without that car so he thought he had me where he wanted me. Well I did not let that stop me. I was driving a car that wouldn't go backwards so I had to make sure I parked so I could always keep going forward.

On payday my friends and I would go somewhere together on our lunch break. We went to the bank to cash our checks and then we would go get something to eat. Whenever we decided to go through a drive-thru, before pulling in I would say "What lane because you know we can't go backwards?" Then we would all start laughing. I was driving and they were riding as if it was a new car.

I drove the car every place I needed to go, as if it was working perfectly. I just had the faith that I would be okay, knowing I could always drive forward. If I had only had that kind of faith that I needed in order to leave Hamilton. If I had only tapped into the faith knowing that I would be fine when I left him.

My mother would say "You better stop driving everywhere in that car. It needs to be fixed."

I would go to the mall and would take long drives just to clear my mind. Long drives and shopping gave me a sense of peace. It helped me stay calm when looking for apartments. I was beginning to get tired of looking. I was looking for a certain type of apartment because of my expensive taste and I knew it would require an expensive budget to pay for it. I finally found some new apartments that were in the process of being built. I really like them and wanted one of them to be my new home.

I filled out an application immediately and it was almost a month later and I still had not heard anything back from the leasing office. In the meantime, I started preparing for the move. I began buying silverware, dishes, shower curtains and other items that I would need for the apartment. I still had not heard anything back from the office, so I went back to the apartments and asked the leasing agent for an update. The agent told me to be patient, it was just taking some time. I told her not to worry about it, I didn't think I was going to be approved for the apartment anyway. I left the office feeling disappointed and I was giving up on the apartment. About two weeks later, they called and informed me that I was approved for the apartment. I went and signed all of the paperwork, picked out my apartment and took my walkthrough to view the apartment. They said I could move in in two weeks.

I was so happy to hear such good news. This made me feel like I was doing the right thing and things were finally working out for me. I told my friends at work and they put in their requests to take off for my move-in date.

I went to the U-Haul rental and rented the truck for the move-in date. I asked the gentleman what time they open and he said 7:30am. I paid in full the cost to reserve the truck for the move-in day and I asked the gentleman if he could possibly get to work at 7 a.m. I informed him it was a matter of life or death and assured him someone would be there to pick up the truck. He assured me that he would not let me down. I went the night before to clean the apartment and started putting up the shower curtains. I cleaned out the refrigerator, wiped down the kitchen cabinets and started putting towels and linen in the linen closet.

The blinds were already put up at every window I put the dishes up in the cabinets. Once I finished cleaning the apartment, I went home and told Hamilton that I was going to do a major cleaning in the house. I took up all the rugs and washed them. I took down the shower curtains as well. Hamilton asked me why I was cleaning so much. I told him the house really needed cleaning. He was intoxicated so he went to bed early. I stayed up washing, folding clothes, packing and placing the Rubbermaid bins back in the garage. I knew he wasn't going to wake up and the kids were asleep as well. This allowed me to work freely in peace and quiet for hours. As I was cleaning, I was imagining that I was washing away the pain and hurt that I had endured in that house. I had prepared for something new and it was now happening. I was cleaning and thanking God.

Although I had the plan in motion, I would not be content until all of my things were placed in the apartment and my kid I were in there safely and securely. I had already taken off my job the next day, so I could take my time and get everything done. I wanted to make sure the move went smoothly and I had to have everything ready to go in the morning. I got up the next morning and put on my scrubs as if I was going to work. On the outside, I was very poised and calm and acted as if it was a normal day. On the inside, I was very anxious and nervous; praying and wanting everything to go over smoothly. I could not take it if anything went wrong with the move. I had to leave Hamilton and this house behind TODAY. I had suffered enough at his hand and now that I had made up my mind and got up the courage to leave it needed to be now. I dropped Andre off at school and Hamilton took London to school.

After dropping Andre off at school I came back home and called my friends and told them that the coast was clear. They went and picked up the U-Haul and everyone met me back at the house. We each had a room to work on and each person worked diligently to complete their assigned room as quickly as possible. They arrived at the house around 8 a.m. and by 9:30 we were finished. We worked both quickly and efficiently, got it done and headed to the apartment. We made it to the apartment, unloaded everything and returned the truck back to U-Haul by 12 noon. I took the time to put every piece of furniture in its appropriate place. By the time I finished, it looked as if I had been living there all the time. I worked until it was time to pick up the kids. I felt so proud of myself. There was a great sense relief and a feeling of accomplishment.

I took a walk through the apartment praying and thanking my father God following allowing me to get everything in and put into place. I was so thankful for having my own place and for having the courage to make the move to get away from Hamilton. I picked up my kids from school and told them we had a new place to live. I told them to let that sink in and we would talk more about it when we got to the apartment. Then I called my attorney and told her she could send the divorce papers to Hamilton. He received them the next day, which was Saturday.

We got settled and I sat down with the kids to have a nice long talk. I said "We are safe now and you no longer have to worry. No one will bother us here. The three of us are going to be a family and we are going to be safe here together." I gave them both big hugs and kisses and told them just how much I loved them.

It took London about a week before she was finally comfortable. She had been living in a great deal of fear, because she was always afraid at the house with Hamilton.

One of my co-workers bought me a king-sized bedroom set and Andre had a queen sized bed. Our apartment only had two bedrooms, so London slept with me. She was still wetting the bed at the time, so I would get her up through the night and take her to the restroom. Finally, she stopped wetting the bed. This was a sure sign that she had finally settled in and was no longer afraid. I reiterated to my kids that they no longer had to be afraid. I would not let anyone hurt them ever again, if I could stop them. I was feeling better and stronger and would do whatever I needed to do in order to protect them.

I was still afraid of Hamilton finding out where we were living because I had no idea what he would do. It was a while before I let him know where I lived, so I would meet him with London at a designated place so that they could see each other. Hamilton was not happy about this and he called his attorney and informed him that I wouldn't allow him to pick London up at the house. This prompted a call from his attorney to my attorney. I then received a call from my attorney stating that as the father Hamilton had some rights.

She said "Ms. Smith, he is within his rights to know where his daughter lives. You can't meet him with her."

I told her that it was just a hard process and I finally gave him the address.

One particular evening, Hamilton brought one of his friends with him to pick up London.

He said "Simone, Hamilton talked about you all the way over here in the car. Do you think the two of you will get back together?"

I looked at his friend and just smiled and shook my head NO! I said to myself what do I look like going back into a tornado that the Lord brought me out of. I tested Hamilton and I knew he had not changed. I could always get under his skin. When the devil tries to take you to hell with him, you know he is no good for you. When he was upset and it was time for him to pick up London, he would call her and tell her that he couldn't make it. She was disappointed because she would have her clothes packed and ready. I would then go into the bedroom, into my closet and close the door.

I would then call Hamilton and ask why he wasn't picking London up and he would say he didn't feel like it.

One day I said "Let me tell you something, our baby is sitting here waiting on you, and you have disappointed her. You don't ever have to bring your butt over here ever again. She has a clean house, a bed to sleep in, and food to eat and has lots of love. If you don't show up, don't ever come back over here! What you won't do is break her heart. She does not need to come to your nasty house anyway. You sorry bastard!"
Well to my knowledge, when I left out of the room London received a phone call. She came to me and said "Daddy said he is coming to get me."

I said "What? Mmmm that's nice. Go and re-brush your teeth." She lit up like a lightbulb. Hamilton tried everything to get me back.

He called with a sad story, telling me that he had cancer and his back had been bothering him. I told him to go to the doctor. He asked if I could go with him and of course I told him no, I didn't think so. It turned out that he did not have cancer.

Imagine me driving that car that would not go into reverse for so long. It amazed me that I was able to drive it so long without getting stranded. I had to keep it moving and I knew I could not let the car stop me. When income tax season came around, I went to the car dealership to look for a car. I was praying that I would be able to get my first car in my own name. I found a Chevrolet Malibu and was able to purchase it. I was extremely happy. When I got home, I prayed, cried, thanked God and prayed some more. I knew, without a shadow of doubt, that the Lord brought me out.

I had escaped the abusive relationship, gotten my apartment and now I had my car. I suffered for so long and now all kinds of doors were being opened for me. It was as if my stepping out on faith and finding the strength to leave Hamilton made the way for my blessings to flow. I told my Heavenly Father that he loves his daughter so well and I thanked him for making me step out on faith and for giving me the strength to be Simone again.

Can you imagine keeping the abuse a secret for so long the way I did? I lived each day not knowing whether I was going to make it or not. I was afraid for my life. Afraid to stay and yet afraid to leave, but the Lord carried me through it. I can say once I left I never looked back and going back was not an option. My divorce was final nine months later.

Out of sheer spite, Hamilton requested that we have a DNA test done. He said that he wanted proof that London was his before he paid me any child support. I couldn't believe he tried to say that London was not his child. The DNA test was taken and the results came back showing 99.99% that she was his.

I told him "You knew she was yours, but you just wanted to be low down and trifling!"

When I moved into my new apartment, I got stronger and very independent. I was already strong and independent, but I had lost those qualities and became very insecure and unsure of myself while I was with Hamilton. After leaving him, I was able to find myself and allow Simone to live again! I was happy go lucky and peaceful again. Leaving Hamilton marked a big turning point in my life. I was finally free; free to live, free to be happy and free to be me!

I became so strong willed that I turned good men away. I was just scared to be hurt again. I felt I just needed to spend some time with myself. One evening, I went to happy hour all by myself. I went to hear the band play. I was a little nervous about going alone, but I did not let it stop me. I walked right in with my head held high and acted as if I meant to be there alone. I sat at the table with people that I didn't know and waited anxiously for the band to come out.

A gentleman came over and said "Excuse me, is anyone sitting here?"

I said "No".

He then offered to buy me a drink and I kindly accepted.

He then asked "Do you come here often?"

I said "Not ever alone, but I usually come here with my girlfriends."

Finally telling me that his name was Tyler, he asked me to dance. We danced and talked, until I finally told him I was going to leave. He decided to leave as well. He walked me to my car and asked if it would be ok for him to call me sometime. I said sure and gave him my phone number. I left and went home and he called me that same night. We began to talk often and got to know each other. I found out that he worked for the Fire Department and seemed to be a very sincere person. He told me that he and his mother usually take a trip to Washington every year in July. His sisters lived there and they would go to visit them, but now that we had met, he said he really did not want to go. When the time came, he went to Washington for a week, and he called me every night while he was there.

During a conversation, Tyler informed me that he likes to get to know a person for at least one month before he consents to helping them pay any bills. I had never asked him for anything and I really did not intend to ask him for money. I told him that I had gone through an ugly divorce and really wasn't looking for anyone right now. We had just started learning and getting to know one another and quite frankly, I was afraid. My kids had just become comfortable and were no longer afraid and I had them to think of, even over myself at that time. Tyler had never been married and had no children.

After we had been seeing each other for about a month, Tyler asked me how much my daughter's tuition was at school. I told him and he said that he would like to give me the money to pay for it every two weeks. At that point, he began helping me pay my bills.

I had trouble believing that it was real. He then asked me for a key to my apartment and I expressed to him that I wasn't sure about giving him a key. He explained that he was not trying to move in but he just wanted to help me. After hesitating, I gave him a key. One day when the kids and I got home from work and school, he had been to the apartment. The refrigerator was full of food and the walk-in pantry was stocked with food. He was not there and when I mentioned it to him, he said "Well you and the kids have to eat." Tyler was so good to me and my kids. My son, Andre even liked him. I have always been drawn to intelligent men, and Tyler was definitely intelligent. As our relationship progressed, I introduced him to my mother and my aunt. Tyler would do thoughtful things like come by my job, pick up my car and take it to have it detailed; he would watch the kids while I went to get my hair done.

He was just too good to be true. He was a great conversationalist and we would talk on the phone for hours.

Tyler was still living at home taking care of his mother. He told me he wanted me to meet his mother, so one day I went by his house to meet her. He introduced us and she was not very friendly. I understood; Tyler was her only son. She loved him dearly and was protective of him. We planned to go out to dinner together with his mother. We set a date and they came to pick me up. After seeing them, I felt I may have been a little overdressed. I was wearing a gray suit with high heel shoes.

Dinner was nice and we all enjoyed it. Tyler dropped me off and they went home. After taking his mom home, Tyler came back over and we sat and talked some more.

He stated that when they got home his mom asked him "Will you be able to handle her? She is a sharp dresser."

He responded "Yes, Simone is a very sweet young lady that takes care of herself and of her two beautiful kids. I watch how she interacts with them and she is a loving mother."

Tyler and his family were planning a wedding anniversary for his aunt and uncle. On that special day, I attended the event and it was very elegant and beautiful. I had the opportunity to meet his sisters and other family members. His family is a very loving family and I had a wonderful time. One day Tyler asked me to call and wake him up when I got off from work around 5:30pm. He said that if he doesn't answer on his cell, then call the house phone. I followed his instructions and called his cell first. When he didn't answer, I called the house phone. His mother answered the phone.

I told her who I was and she said that he was not home. His mother was very protective of him. I called Tyler by his last name instead of his first name and she was quick to correct me. She adamantly informed me that his name was "Tyler". I respectfully said "thank you" and hung up the phone. About 10 minutes later Tyler called me and asked why I didn't call to wake him up as he had asked. I told him that I did and his mother answered and said that he was not there. He had me repeat what I said so that he could be sure that he heard me correctly. The answer made him very angry. He told me to hold on and said to his mother "Did you tell Simone that I was not here?"

She said "Yes" He asked "Mama why would you do that, that was rude!"
Tyler then told me that he would call me back.

He reminded her that he was staying there to help her because he didn't want her living there alone. He told his mother that she has to stop treating him like a child because he is a grown man and is no longer her little boy. Tyler apologized to me for what his mother said. I told him it was ok. He stated that it was not ok and he did not appreciate her doing that to me. He said she does that all the time. She even tried to intercept calls from his friends. He told his mom that if she kept doing that he was going to get his own place. I am not sure what she was trying to accomplish by intercepting calls from others. I guess she wanted him all to herself and did not want to share his attention with anyone else. It sounded as if he was pretty upset about it and she was risking him moving out which would have been a lot worse than sharing some of his time.

Tyler was very good to me and my kids and he was always willing to help me. We would take the kids out to the movies or to dinner. Whenever his schedule would permit, he would pick London up from school. This would help me on the days that I had to take Andre to tutoring at McDonalds. McDonalds had a free tutoring program. They had retired teachers come in and tutor children after school. Later, I decided to enroll London as well. The teachers admired me for taking out the time to sit and wait on my kids patiently. I just wanted to make sure they were listening and obeying the teacher. I admired the teachers because they tutored each child on different levels. Each teacher had about five to six students to a table and there were four teachers. The teachers taught each student based on their learning style.

I really appreciated this because each child learns differently and often times in a classroom the teachers teach all of the students using the same method. McDonalds did a great job teaching my kids and I appreciate them.

Andre walked away with a formula for math that will stick with him and that he can carry with him throughout his life. She told me if he remembers this formula, he will master math. London was already excellent in math, but they strengthened her on her comprehension skills. When riding in the car, my kids and I would always play the alphabet game. We would see how many words we could say starting with the first letter of the alphabet, the second letter, and so on all the way to the letter Z. I would also give my children math problems, while cooking dinner.

Education was important to me and I took every opportunity to help them advance in their studies. I stressed to them that education was one of the very important keys to success. They seemed to enjoy school which was a good thing.

As time went on, I realized that Tyler and I seemed to be drifting apart. Our relationship seemed to be almost nonexistent. After talking for a year and a half, we decided to call it off. He said he needed someone to show him affection and I was unable to do that. I felt really bad that I was unable to give him that one thing he needed when he had done so much for me and my kids. There was a new song out on the radio at that time and the lyrics were:

"When a woman's fed up
There is nothing you can do about it."

I was fed up with Hamilton and I was having a hard time accepting love from Tyler. I realized that I had let a great man go. You don't find many men that accept your two small children and treat them so well. My son, Andre had really become fond of Tyler and opened up to him. He helped Andre with his math often. No matter how great I knew he was and how well he treated me, I just could not tear the wall down that I had built to guard and protect my heart. It had been so high and strong that Tyler could not compete with it and I know I missed out on a lot. My heart had not quite healed from all of the inflicted pain and abuse in which I had been subjected to in my previous marriage. I still needed to be delivered and escape the darkness and come into the light.

Tyler had been too good to me and I certainly never wanted to hurt him or make him suffer for the terrible things that Hamilton had done, so I had to release him. I still think about Tyler sometimes even now and I will forever be grateful to him and remember how great of a man he was.

Thanks be unto to God our Father. I was starting my life all over again and I am glad about it. I had stepped out on Faith and that took a great deal of courage. I was able to leave a man that abused me for eight years. I had to recondition my body and mind, meaning I had to get it out of the state in which it was used to being. I had to remind myself that the mind controls the body and I had to be careful what I allowed my mind to think because it would affect my behavior. I also had to watch what I was putting in my body. This was a low period in my life with Hamilton.

I suffered from a deep depression. The longer I was away from him, the more confident I became. As time progressed, I became more and more happier with myself and with my life. When I saw the smiles on my kid's faces, it melted my heart and reminded me why I did what I did. I just wanted them to be happy and I allowed them little privileges. For instance, I let them snack on whatever they liked, as long as they ate their dinner. Tyler would still call periodically to check and see how the kids and I were doing. I thought this was very sweet of him; again this was a testament as to how thoughtful he was.

About four months later, my girlfriend, Swann was telling me about her cousin who was a nurse and trained dogs. He started working at the hospital.

I saw him one day and he said hello, but I did not stop to talk to him because I was heading out on my lunch break to eat and to run some errands. Finally, the next morning, Swann and I met for breakfast in the cafeteria. She told me that her cousin was supposed to meet her for breakfast. I told her okay and he came and joined us. I acknowledged that I saw him the day before. He introduced himself and wanted to know if he could meet me every morning for breakfast. I said sure. He came and knocked on my office door around 7:15am and we went to the cafeteria for breakfast. We started getting to know each other. He finally asked me if he could take me to dinner. I agreed to have dinner with him and he came to the apartment and picked me up. We went out and ordered our food, picked it up and brought it back to my place to eat. My phone started ringing off the hook.

It was Hamilton and I asked what he wanted because I had company. He was so angry and kept calling me every five minutes.

Hamilton said "Oh now you got you a man?"

I was initially answering the phone because I thought there may have been an emergency. Besides the gentleman and I was just sitting and talking. He kept calling all night and I kept hanging up on him. I told him if he didn't stop calling me, I would change my number and call my attorney and tell him he was harassing me. He finally stopped calling. The gentleman that I was with probably thought I was dealing with a maniac and did not want to get involved. However, we were just friends anyway and that is all I wanted it to be between us. He seemed very nice, but I already knew I was not interested and I was not going to talk to him. He had large dogs in his home and I had a problem with that.

He let them ride in the truck with him as well. I was not that comfortable with dogs and I definitely did not want them in the house or in the car with me. As a result, I would never get out of my car and go inside his house and I would never ride in his truck; that was a little too close for comfort. The dogs were a big turn off for me. I was very open and honest with him, as I would want someone to be with me. I told him that it wasn't going to work out with us and I did not want to pursue a relationship with him, but we could be friends. He was a very nice guy but he was not for me.

He said "Hot Damn, I can't change your mind?"

I said "I'm sorry, but no." We eventually stopped talking. I started throwing myself into my work, exercising and going out with the girls.

Whenever the girls and I would hang out, we liked to go to happy hour and then hang around and listen to the band that was performing. I would have drinks coming from everywhere. I believe my confidence level had gone up a few notches. I was much happier with myself and it was showing through. Men find a confident woman more attractive than a woman that is insecure and lacks self-love and self-confidence. As a result of my being confident, men were attracted to me and were happy to buy me drinks, whenever I went out. I never asked for them.

One particular night, we went to happy hour to celebrate one of my girlfriend's birthday. There was about 15 of us. We were all drinking, talking, laughing and having a great time. As I was enjoying the girls, I was also scanning the room and observing my surroundings as I usually do.

While scanning the room, I noticed a gentleman standing on the wall, looking over at our table. I was wondering who he was looking at. I looked at everyone at the table and said "Who is he looking at". They didn't know either. I told Swann that I needed to go to the ladies' room. On the way to the ladies' room, I passed directly by the gentleman standing on the wall. He touched me, smiled and said hi. I said to myself, it was me that he was looking at. When I returned to the table, I told Swann that the gentleman who was staring at our table was looking at me.

Swann said "I knew that. Simone, you are gorgeous girl! Plus you have on that pretty, short dress." I just smiled. It was Swann that always told me that I was beautiful. I never thought I was and realized that I needed to be reminded that I was beautiful.

After dealing with Hamilton for so long, I had begun to feel that I was not the person that I knew I was. Everyone needs someone in their life to speak into them and remind them who they are. Swann was that person for me and I was grateful to have her.

Some of the girls had to leave and were only planning to stay for happy hour. They left to go home and the rest of us decided to move on upstairs and listen to the band. As we headed upstairs, I looked behind me and there was the gentleman coming up the stairs behind us.

Swann said "I don't know why he is coming upstairs. He's not buying any drinks."

I said "He did ask if I wanted something to drink." He finally came over and asked me to dance and I agreed.

As we were dancing, he was smiling from ear to ear. After we danced, he came over and sat at the table with us. I introduced him to everyone at the table and we talked. He bought a round of drinks for the entire table. I looked over at Swann and smiled. I was thinking, here is your drink Swann. The two of us went out on several dates and had a great time. I then found out that he was married. That was the end of that. I don't play with nobody's husband. A covenant should be honored and respected. I was angry and hurt about not having a choice in whether or not my husband was out seeing other women, when we were together, and I was certainly not going to share someone else's husband. This type of situation always proves to be a lose-lose situation.

I began to pray more and make necessary attempts to get closer to my Heavenly Father.

I was so happy again knowing that my God had been taking such good care of us. My son and daughter were happy. I decided to work and enjoy my kids and give my mind a rest. I acknowledged that I did not need any foolishness in my life. I remained active in the church and would exercise and go out with the girls from time to time. This was what I needed. When someone has been in an abusive relationship or any failed relationship, they need to spend time alone and get to know themselves again. I was finally finding me. I needed to rediscover my likes and dislikes, my dreams and get to know me again. I had been subjected to Hamilton's control over me and needed to enjoy my newfound freedom without the concern of a man's needs and wants. I was mistreated because he was insecure.

If you are in an abusive relationship, please understand that you do not have to remain there. If your significant other loves you, they should not want to hurt you. Domestic violence is a twisted love that has tipped the scale of insanity and control. Where do we go from here? Now that you have taken the journey with me through my abusive relationship and my new found freedom, please stay tuned for my next book entitled "*A Dark Cloud*". Look out for the book as it is coming soon! Thanks for your support.

~VJS

www.ingramcontent.com/pod-product-compliance
Lightning Source LLC
Chambersburg PA
CBHW051834090426
42736CB00011B/1800

Finding My Way

My Unspoken Truth is a book that explores secrets, lies and deceit, leading to an emotional and domestically violent relationship of a pregnant woman who suffered abuse by the hands of her husband. Finding a way out is easier said than done when you're in a relationship with someone you love. The hardest part is bringing children into a situation where you are now forced to be someone who can look at it from the outside to see clearly what is happening. A domestically violent relationship usually begins with an emotional tearing apart; ripping away your self-esteem, lowering your self-worth, and finally, physical abuse. After years of abuse Simone finds her way out of what could have cost her her life.

ISBN 9780996722070

90000 >

9 780996 722070